little FAITH book

color me in!

by jennifer lynn

feel free to decorate this page with markers, stickers, washi tape or whatever!

BY JENNIFER LYNN

COVER AND INTERIOR DESIGN BY JENNIFER LYNN
PUBLISHED BY BEN KNISKERN/WRITE IDEA PRESS

FIRST EDITION / MAY 2015

ISBN-13: 978-1512280036
ISBN-10: 1512280038

PRINTED IN THE UNITED STATES OF AMERICA

LITTLEFAITHBLOG.COM

Welcome to your very own Little Faith Book! This journal is for anything and everything related to our awesome God—Bible verses, prayer requests, Christian song lyrics and more!

This is a place where you can use your creativity and craftiness to help build your relationship with Jesus. I encourage you to decorate this book to your heart's content! Express your own unique style on each page with doodles, stickers, scrapbook paper, etc.

Your Little Faith Book is separated into four sections: INSPIRE, STUDY, PRAY and PRAISE. There are suggestions at the beginning of each section to help you get started, but feel free to let your own creativity take over! (Tip: You may want to mark your sections with page markers, washi tape or paper clips so they're easier to find.)

I think you're ready to get started! I truly hope you have a blast digging into God's Word, praying and growing closer to Jesus while using your artsy-ness to honor Him.

To find out more about the Little Faith Book and see how other girls are using theirs, check out:

littlefaithblog.com *and* #littlefaithbook on Instagram

about me

I praise you, for I am fearfully and wonderfully made. Wonderful are your works; my soul knows it very well.
~Psalm 139:14 (ESV)

NAME:

NICKNAME:

AGE:

BIRTHDAY:

SCHOOL:

CHURCH:

place picture
of you here

the hobbies I love are:
(circle ones that apply to you and add your own!)

WRITING   PHOTOGRAPHY   ART   SHOPPING

SINGING   WATCHING NETFLIX

COOKING   TRAVELING   DANCING   BAKING   READING

SPORTS   ACTING   PLAYING AN INSTRUMENT   DIY & CRAFTS

my favorite:

BOOK IN THE BIBLE:

ICE CREAM FLAVOR:

STORE:

CHRISTIAN SINGER/BAND:

VACATION SPOT:

SPORT:

BIBLE CHARACTER:

MOVIE:

SOCIAL MEDIAS:

SEASON:

FOOD:

THEME PARK RIDE:

how I take my coffee:

5 random facts about me:

1.

2.

3.

4.

5.

fill this in with your favorite
COLOR (s)

supply ideas

markers
colored pencils
crayons
paint
watercolors
paintbrushes
card stock paper
scrapbook paper
tape/glue
scissors
pictures
sticky notes
bows
washi tape

paper clips
stapler
flowers
stickers
journaling cards
paint chips
ribbon
string
duct tape
tags
envelopes
glitter
3D stickers
polaroid pictures

For we are God's masterpiece. He has created us anew in Christ
Jesus, so we can do the good things he planned for us long ago.
~Ephesians 2:10

Inspire ♡

for Christian quotes, Christian lyrics, Bible verses, fun journaling prompts, etc. start off by doodling some of your favorite Christian quotes on this page! (and to find ideas and inspiration for this section, check out littlefaithblog.com)

Those who live at the ends of the
earth stand in awe of your wonders.
From where the sun rises to where
it sets, you inspire shouts of joy.
~Psalm 65:8

MY IDEAS
FOR THIS SECTION

doodle your favorite Bible verse.

I ♥ GOD

1.

2.

5.

6.

9.

10.

13.

14.

BECAUSE...

color me in

3.

4.

7.

8.

11.

12.

15.

16.

write Bible verses and encouraging quotes on

paint chips and attach them to these pages.

Thank You

tip: cover these pages with scrapbook paper first!

God For...

make a collage of things you're thankful to God for! you can do this with pictures, drawings, just words, or however you'd like.

doodle lyrics from one of your favorite worship songs.

MAKE A LIST OF YOUR FAVORITE CHRISTIAN ARTISTS.

My Favorite

Bible Verses

a place to write, doodle and keep track of all the verses in the Bible you love the most!

write encouraging messages and verses you'd send to a friend if they were having a bad day.

CHRISTIAN CONCERTS I'VE BEEN TO:

picture from
concert

CHRISTIAN ARTISTS I WANT TO SEE IN CONCERT:

doodle Isaiah 40:8.

press flowers in these pages.

My Testimony

_____

- - - - - - - - - - - - - - - - - - -

- - - - - - - - - - - - - - - - - - -

- - - - - - - - - - - - - - - - - - -

- - - - - - - - - - - - - - - - - - -

- - - - - - - - - - - - - - - - - - -

- - - - - - - - - - - - - - - - - - -

- - - - - - - - - - - - - - - - - - -

- - - - - - - - - - - - - - - - - - -

- - - - - - - - - - - - - - - - - - -

- - - - - - - - - - - - - - - - - - -

- - - - - - - - - - - - - - - - - - -

- - - - - - - - - - - - - - - - - - -

- - - - - - - - - - - - - - - - - - -

- - - - - - - - - - - - - - - - - - -

doodle your life verse.

(THE ONE VERSE IN THE BIBLE THAT SPEAKS
TO YOUR HEART MORE THAN ANY OTHER)

{STUDY} ♥

for daily Bible study, Bible reading plans, devotions, and anything else related to reading and studying the Word.

free monthly Bible reading plans that you can print out and stick in this section are available on littlefaithblog.com!

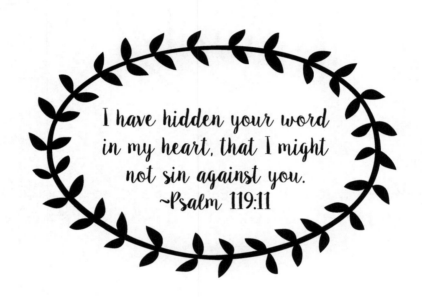

I have hidden your word in my heart, that I might not sin against you.
~Psalm 119:11

BIBLE STUDY TIPS

1. FIND A BIBLE VERSION YOU ENJOY AND UNDERSTAND. MY FAVORITES ARE NLT, ESV AND NCV. IF YOU DON'T HAVE A BIBLE OR AREN'T ABLE TO BUY ONE RIGHT NOW, THERE ARE OODLES OF FREE WEBSITES WHERE YOU CAN READ THE BIBLE ONLINE! THE YOUVERSION BIBLE APP IS AMAZING, AND BIBLE HUB AND BIBLE GATEWAY ARE GREAT BIBLE WEBSITES.

2. GET A DEVOTIONAL BOOK OR FIND FREE DEVOTIONS ONLINE. (YOU CAN READ DEVOTIONS ON MY BLOG AND ON MY INSTAGRAM, @CHRISTIANGIRLS. CHECK OUT THESE HASHTAGS ON INSTAGRAM: #BLOOMTOWARDGOD, #DISNEYDEVOLAND, #DFHDISNEY AND #FALLININBIBLESTUDY.) JUST BE VERY CAREFUL THAT ANY DEVOTIONAL YOU USE AGREES WITH THE BIBLE.

3. MAKE IT FUN! IF YOU ENJOY JUST READING THE BIBLE BY ITSELF, THAT'S AWESOME. BUT FOR ME, I LOVE TO GET OUT ALL MY MARKERS, HIGHLIGHTERS, STICKERS, ETC. AND MARK MY BIBLE UP! I HIGHLIGHT, UNDERLINE OR BOX IN ANY VERSES THAT STAND OUT TO ME AND MAKE DOODLES AND NOTES EVERYWHERE. IT'S MADE BIBLE STUDY SO MUCH MORE ENJOYABLE FOR ME! "DIRTY BIBLE, CLEAN CHRISTIAN."

4. FIND A TIME OF DAY THAT WORKS BEST FOR YOU AND DO YOUR DEVOTIONS EVERY DAY AT THAT TIME. AFTER A WHILE IT WILL BECOME A HABIT. I LIKE TO DO MY DEVOTIONS FIRST THING IN THE MORNING (SOMETIMES WITH A CUP OF COFFEE), BUT FIND WHAT WORKS BEST FOR YOU!

cover this page with scrapbook paper and stick
a Bible reading plan for this month here! ♡

day 1

DATE: _____

PASSAGE: _____

What is this passage saying?

_____

_____

_____

What verse really stood out to you? Feel free to doodle it!

How can you take what you learned in this passage and make it a part of your life?

_____

_____

_____

topics I'd like to study:

As you study the Bible, use the following pages to record verses that relate to a specific topic, such as love, depression, self-esteem, etc.

VERSES ON
love ♡

P.S. (these pages don't have to be completed all at once! you can add verses as you come across them over time.)

John 3:16

1 Corinthians 13

1 John 4:8

VERSES ON
depression

Psalm 147:3
1 Peter 5:7
Psalm 56:8

VERSES ON
self-esteem

Psalm 139:13-14
1 Peter 3:3-4
Luke 12:7

VERSES ON

VERSES ON

VERSES ON

VERSES ON

But you must remain faithful to the things you have been taught. You know they are true, for you know you can trust those who taught you. You have been taught the holy Scriptures from childhood, and they have given you the wisdom to receive the salvation that comes by trusting in Christ Jesus. All Scripture is inspired by God and is useful to teach us what is true and to make us realize what is wrong in our lives. It corrects us when we are wrong and teaches us to do what is right. God uses it to prepare and equip his people to do every good work.

~2 Timothy 3:14-17

sermon notes

date: _____   speaker: _____

topic: _____

message: _____

_____

_____

_____

_____

_____

_____

_____

_____

_____

_____

_____

_____

_____

_____

_____

_____

_____

_____

_____

_____

sermon notes

date: _____   speaker: _____

topic: _____

message: _____

_____

_____

_____

_____

_____

_____

_____

_____

_____

_____

_____

_____

_____

_____

_____

_____

_____

_____

_____

_____

sermon notes

date: _____   speaker: _____

topic: _____

message: _____

_____

_____

_____

_____

_____

_____

_____

_____

_____

_____

_____

_____

_____

_____

_____

_____

_____

_____

_____

_____

_____

_____

sermon notes

date: _____   speaker: _____

topic: _____

message: _____

_____

_____

_____

_____

_____

_____

_____

_____

_____

_____

_____

_____

_____

_____

_____

_____

_____

_____

_____

_____

_____

sermon notes

date: _____   speaker: _____

topic: _____

message: _____

_____

_____

_____

_____

_____

_____

_____

_____

_____

_____

_____

_____

_____

_____

_____

_____

_____

_____

_____

_____

_____

sermon notes

date: _____   speaker: _____

topic: _____

message: _____

_____

_____

_____

_____

_____

_____

_____

_____

_____

_____

_____

_____

_____

_____

_____

_____

_____

_____

_____

_____

_____

sermon notes

date: _____   speaker: _____

topic: _____

message: _____

_____

_____

_____

_____

_____

_____

_____

_____

_____

_____

_____

_____

_____

_____

_____

_____

_____

_____

_____

_____

sermon notes

date: _____   speaker: _____

topic: _____

message: _____

_____

_____

_____

_____

_____

_____

_____

_____

_____

_____

_____

_____

_____

_____

_____

_____

_____

_____

_____

_____

_____

sermon notes

date: _____   speaker: _____

topic: _____

message: _____
_____
_____
_____
_____
_____
_____
_____
_____
_____
_____
_____
_____
_____
_____
_____
_____
_____
_____
_____
_____
_____
_____
_____

sermon notes

date: _____   speaker: _____

topic: _____

message: _____

----

sermon notes

date: _____   speaker: _____

topic: _____

message: _____
_____
_____
_____
_____
_____
_____
_____
_____
_____
_____
_____
_____
_____
_____
_____
_____
_____
_____
_____
_____
_____
_____
_____

sermon notes

date: _____   speaker: _____

topic: _____

message: _____
_____
_____
_____
_____
_____
_____
_____
_____
_____
_____
_____
_____
_____
_____
_____
_____
_____
_____
_____
_____
_____
_____

pray

for prayer
requests and
written prayers
to God.

(tip: find prayer requests from girls
like you and submit your own at the
Prayer Corner on littlefaithblog.com)

Rejoice in our confident
hope. Be patient in trouble,
and keep on praying.
~Romans 12:12

PEOPLE to PRAY for:

PRRR-AYER GUIDE

C ONFESSION. CONFESS YOUR SINS TO GOD AND ASK FOR HIS FORGIVENESS.

A DORATION. WORSHIP, PRAISE AND ADORE GOD FOR WHO HE IS AND WHAT HE'S DONE.

T HANKSGIVING. THANK GOD FOR THE MANY BLESSINGS HE'S GIVEN YOU.

S UPPLICATION. BRING YOUR NEEDS AND CARES TO GOD, AS WELL AS THE NEEDS OF OTHERS.

Dear God,

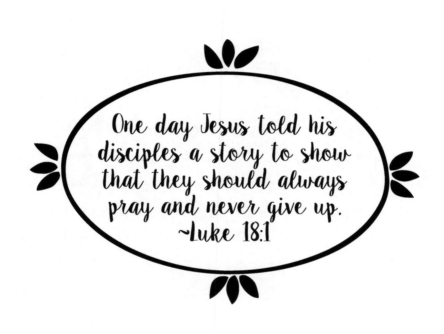

One day Jesus told his disciples a story to show that they should always pray and never give up.
~Luke 18:1

Jot down Matthew 6:9-13.

I said to the LORD, "You are my Master! Every good thing I have comes from you."
-Psalm 16:2

PRAISE

a place to list all the blessings in your life.

1. God's love ♡♡
2. Jesus dying for me
3.

tip: make two columns
for more space!

"LET EVERYTHING THAT BREATHES SING PRAISES TO THE LORD! PRAISE THE LORD!"
PSALM 150:6 ♡

"LET ALL THAT I AM PRAISE THE LORD; WITH MY WHOLE HEART, I WILL PRAISE HIS HOLY NAME. LET ALL THAT I AM PRAISE THE LORD; MAY I NEVER FORGET THE GOOD THINGS HE DOES FOR ME."
PSALM 103:1-2 ♡

"THEN MY TONGUE SHALL TELL
OF YOUR RIGHTEOUSNESS AND OF
YOUR PRAISE ALL THE DAY LONG."
PSALM 35:28 (ESV) ♡

ALSO AVAILABLE FROM JENNIFER LYNN

Little Faith Book
(Create Your Own Cover)

LET'S KEEP IN TOUCH!

 littlefaithblog.com

 @christiangirls

 booksandjesus

Made in the USA
San Bernardino, CA
15 September 2017